NOW YOU CAN READ ABOUT...
DINOSAURS

TEXT BY HARRY STANTON

ILLUSTRATED BY BOB HERSEY

BRIMAX BOOKS · NEWMARKET · ENGLAND

Dinosaur means terrible lizard. They were the largest animals to have walked on the earth. The largest dinosaurs weighed up to fifty tonnes and were about twenty five metres long.

No one ever saw
a dinosaur.
Dinosaurs died
out long before
there were ever
any men or women
on the earth.

Each Brontosaurus dinosaur weighed as much as six elephants.

Brontosaurus stayed together in herds because they were attacked by meat eating dinosaurs.

Brontosaurus
(Bron-toh-sawrus)

The largest dinosaurs were the Diplodocus. They were as long as three railway coaches. They were able to raise their heads very high so that they could eat leaves from the tops of trees.

Diplodocus
(Dip-lod-oh-cus)

Some of them did not eat plants. These were the meat eating dinosaurs. They ate other dinosaurs.

Tyrannosaurus Rex
(Ty-ran-oh-sawrus Rex)

The Tyrannosaurus Rex were the largest of the meat eating dinosaurs. They stood on their back legs and were over six metres high. They weighed eight tonnes. Tyrannosaurus Rex had long sharp teeth and very short arms.

Many plant eating dinosaurs ran away when they were attacked. But some who were slow moving had armour.

Stegosaurus was as long as a bus. On its back it had two rows of bony plates for armour. There were no plates on its side to protect it.

Stegosaurus
(Steg-oh-sawrus)

Ankylosaurus
(An-kyle-oh-sawrus)

The flat back of the
Ankylosaurus was covered
in armour.

Look at the bony club at
the end of its tail. It
could use the club if it
had to fight other dinosaurs.

These strange bone-headed
dinosaurs had very thick
skulls. The bone of their
skulls was over twenty
five centimetres thick.
This protected them when
they fought.

Look at the long horn which the Parasaurolophus had on the back of their heads. They ate leaves with jaws that looked like a duck's beak. Inside their jaws they had hundreds of small sharp teeth. Unlike you and I when the teeth wore down they grew new ones.

Parasaurolophus
(Para-saw-roh-loh-fus)

Triceratops
(Try-sair-oh-tops)

The Triceratops had three very long horns. One on its nose and one over each eye. Covering its neck it had a shield of bone. Triceratops had flat teeth to help it eat tough leaves.

Another horned dinosaur was the Styracosaurus. It had a horn on its nose seventy centimetres long. Its head was over two metres long and it weighed three and a half tonnes.

Styracosaurus
(Sty-rak-oh-sawrus)

Horned dinosaurs ate plants. With their sharp horns they charged any other dinosaurs that attacked them.

At the same time as the
dinosaurs, strange creatures
hunted in the sea.
Ichthyosaurs means fish
lizard. It had sharp teeth and
large eyes.
Plesiosaurs were
about twelve metres long.
They had large flat flippers
and very long necks.

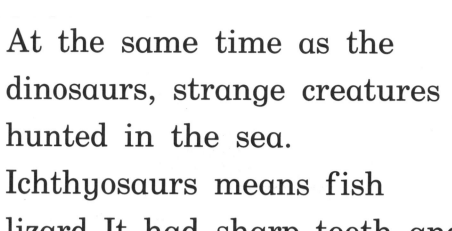

Plesiosaurs
(*Ples-e-oh-saws*)

Ichthyosaurs
(*Ik-thee-oh-saws*)

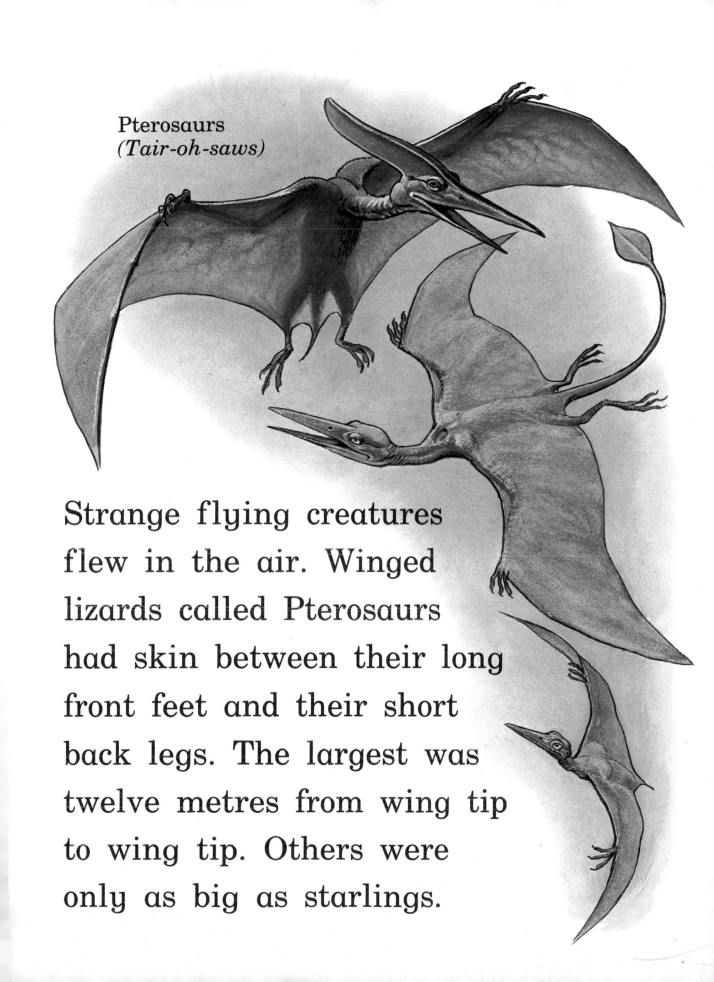

Pterosaurs
(Tair-oh-saws)

Strange flying creatures flew in the air. Winged lizards called Pterosaurs had skin between their long front feet and their short back legs. The largest was twelve metres from wing tip to wing tip. Others were only as big as starlings.

The age of dinosaurs came to an end.
All the dinosaurs died out when
the earth became cooler about
sixty five million years ago.
This did not happen suddenly. It
took thousands of years.

Perhaps it was too cold for them to live or perhaps their food did not grow.
Even the strange creatures that flew in the air and those that swam in the sea died out.

The bones of some
dinosaurs can still
be found today.
When some of the
creatures died they
fell into soft mud.
This mud gradually
hardened. The bones
then became fossils
and the mud around
them hardened into
rock.

Some fossils are found when the rock is worn away. Other fossils are found in mines or stone quarries.

What are the names of these Dinosaurs?

Brontosaurus

Stegosaurus

Styracosaurus

Parasaurolophus

Pterosaurs

Tyrannosaurus Rex